This Volume
is presented
in Loving Memory of

_____

by

_____

_____

_____

_____

Date

Beyond This Day

Text

John Sidney Tighe

Original Art and Art Direction

Christopher Pelicano

Graphic Design and Layout

Ron Mahannah
Marcia Bousquet

Production

Lewis Holland

Dedication

To all those who have walked with Sorrow...
and passed her lessons on.

© MM

PRINTED IN THE U.S.A..

GOOD WILL PUBLISHERS, INC.

Beyond This Day

The Way of Hope

...Bereavement is a universal and integral part of our experience of love.
— *C.S. Lewis*

The Purpose and Use of this Book

This volume is designed as a keepsake and a tribute. It is a tribute to your recently deceased loved one, a document of your love and remembrance for someone special. It is also a keepsake in which you are invited to record family history through a family chart and through selected journal entries relating to your life with your loved one and others. In a way this book is a celebration, a celebration of human connectedness and sacrifice, a celebration of commitment and of love. It may, if you choose to use it as such, help you come to grips with the deep sorrow that accompanies a death in the family. It may actually help you in your grief, for grief is a process and healthy aids in that process can be invaluable.

You may choose to use this volume in different ways and at different times, just as we all experience our sorrow in our own special way and in our own time. However you choose to use your volume, it is meant as a reflection of a strong belief that memorialization is a natural component of human behavior and can therefore help us through difficult times. It is the sincere desire of the publisher and the donors of this volume that in some small way we may, in the gift that is this lovely book, touch your heart in a time when so many of us feel so alone. We hope this keepsake tribute will help you celebrate a particular life, as well as life itself. We believe you are worth the time and the energy it takes to say, "Hang in there, friend, you are in our thoughts."

So use your volume as you wish, it exists for your comfort, consolation and hope. May all our lives serve as tributes to those who have passed before us, ever recalling the love that was shared so that we, in turn, may pass it on to all our dear loved ones. This passing on of love through families and friends and people with whom we come into contact is, indeed, the way of hope and the secret to life everlasting.

Beyond This Day

We know that any individual's mortality is inextricably bound to other humans, for we are social creatures; we live in groups and usually do what we can to make the life of the group a little better for our having been a part of it. Our particular effect on those around us is a kind of immortality. If, for instance, a child learns to appreciate the inestimable value of a good book, of education or of true friends, and cultivates that appreciation throughout life; if indeed that appreciation is then passed on to another generation of offspring, a sort of memory is in process. Life is continuing… beyond this moment, beyond this hour, beyond this day. The title of our book, *Beyond This Day*, is simply an affirmation that we are not alone, that in the act of sharing or relating in a positive way we have given a keepsake to those we love.

It is not only by our specific actions that we can make a difference in people's lives, but also by our presence. We share who we are with others. And over time, we will have either a positive or a negative effect on the people we know. We will either genuinely care for others or succumb to our own self-centeredness. We determine this. We will, at least to a certain degree, fashion some of the emotional experiences of those close to us, experiences that will naturally continue in their memories long after we are gone.

And so is the case with those who have passed before us. Quite often it is a fondness and deep regard for one close to us, cultivated over the course of the relationship, that we remember and put to good use in our lives long after that loved one is no longer here. Even where there was discord, we can usually find a kernel of positive influence having flowed from a deceased friend or family member. We came to realize that the positive influence of those who have gone before us exists beyond the present, and the love engendered by them certainly exists… beyond this day.

Part One:

Remembering

*"We are put on earth a little space
that we may learn to bear the beams of love."*
—Charles Baudelaire

The Great Longing

Throughout recorded history humankind has grieved the passing of one of its own. The very first cultures surely found ways to mitigate the sorrow suffered by various members of the clan. As cultures grew and civilization expanded, peoples of the world began to tie their grief to their particular belief systems. And so a deceased loved one came to live with the Great Spirit, or found Enlightenment, experienced Nirvana or traveled to Heaven. Peoples of the world have variously defined the great longing in the human heart to reach beyond. Because of the inevitability of death, the act of remembering deceased loved ones has always been a way to hold the life of another in our minds. In this way memory is a great teacher. The notion that a loved one remains with us in some capacity after death is an old idea which today is understood in a variety of ways. Though it is defined differently in different belief systems, what we share as humans is the innate need, the *great longing* to memorialize those we have loved and to recognize the spiritual component of grieving their loss.

Remembering our loved ones is a deeply felt, essentially celebratory process. The more life has been shared the more indescribable the sorrow that is encountered when a loved one passes away. But the sharing need not stop, for the particular qualities that endeared a loved one to us can and should be passed on to others, either within the family or outside the family. Our loved ones live on in the hearts and minds of those who are left. The *great longing* is really for an undying connection to those we love. The goodness they engendered does not perish, but lives in the acts of those who witnessed that goodness and learned something from it.

A Tribute

In this section you are invited to remember your loved one in some very special ways. A record of the funeral service itself is provided for those who, in years to come, will see how, when and where you bade your loved one farewell. A place for a photograph of the deceased will, of course, become one of the family treasures you pass on. Next you will find a place to list some very special friends who attended the funeral. A place is also provided to list friends who were near and dear to you in a difficult time. Special times with your loved ones are precious memories. Your recollections in the *Times I Will Always Remember* section may someday provide for family members an inspirational keepsake unlike any other. Adding a reminiscence of your family life to this very personal documentation is a befitting testimonial to one you have loved and will remember always.

The Funeral Service

for

_____

Service

_____
LOCATION

_____
OFFICIATING

_____
DATE

Cemetery

_____
CEMETERY NAME

_____
DATE OF INTERMENT   SECTION   LOT

A Tribute

Place Picture Here

Special Friends
in Attendance

_____

_____

_____

_____

_____

_____

_____

_____

_____

_____

_____

_____

_____

_____

_____

_____

_____

_____

_____

_____

_____

Friends for Life
and More...

Some friends are just always there for us, aren't they? What would we ever do without them? They have given us such joy in their presence, their humor, their forbearance. They have made the good times better and the bad times more bearable. They have ventured closer to us because of their honesty and their caring. They have risked ill feeling by cracking through our walls and really getting to know us. In truth, they have loved us, even when we weren't completely lovable!

For these friends how can we show our appreciation? What can we do to pay them back? No recompense is ever adequate, of course, for true friendship is invaluable. We may only thank them by our resolve to live the fullness of our lives, even in our deep pain, even in our grief.

We list those friends here, those who brought food or spent time with us, those whose flowers we will always remember, those whose notes, even from out of town, touched us in special ways. We list the friends for whom we know we can count on for comfort and for consolation, the ones who have been and will continue to be with us for life, for death and for all the in-betweens.

Those Near and Dear

_____

_____

_____

_____

_____

_____

_____

_____

_____

_____

_____

_____

The Stream of Time

"Time is but the stream I go a fishing in."
—Henry David Thoreau

Thoreau, in his brief quote, described well the act of remembering. How wonderful the gift of memory can be when sweet recollections help heal our aching hearts. How therapeutic it can be to cast a line of memory into the stream of time and pull up hallowed moments. The remarkable endeavors, the prominent desires, the cherished dreams, fulfilled or not, are all the ingredients of an individual's life worth speaking of, worth citing for those left behind.

In this section you may journey back to your first meeting with a loved one. The reminiscence may contain a foreshadowing of your future together, perhaps a whimsical banter, or a curious intimation of the deep feeling to come. There is usually in the record of a first meeting between couples who will spend their lives together, or between parent and newborn child or among closest friends, some semblance of awe and respect flowing from one heart to another, some initial longing for togetherness that is well worth retrieving from the recesses of the mind. We have provided here a few pages for more of that journey back to a former time: a survey of a year or a snapshot of a moment, a description of a memorable event or a few written words as witness to a blessed history. It is yours for the writing, your stream in which to drop a line.

Times I Will
Always Remember

_____

_____

_____

_____

_____

_____

_____

_____

_____

_____

_____

_____

_____

_____

_____

_____

_____

_____

_____

_____

_____

_____

Our Family Tree

It has been a long standing tradition in families to keep track of ancestors and descendents by making a record of them in a family keepsake. Most families have one or more people who delve into the genealogical records and try to keep tabs on who is who in the family. These folks usually become repositories of family stories as well as archivists of sorts with their collections of family photographs and memorabilia. Invaluable to our family "watchers" and other family members as well are the keepsakes passed down through generations. Personal family keepsakes make genealogists of us all, for a treasured keepsake is a record of the heart, tracking the virtues and the character that make families special.

In the following section you are invited to trace your roots in a way that may someday be handed down to an interested family member. Family histories always remind us of the continuity of life and therefore how blessed we are with family. We hope that you are able at some time to find strength in your family tree, for it can serve as a chronicle of love to help you live through the sorrow that is now a part of that love.

Family Register

Marriage

DATE ———————— WHERE

SPOUSE

DATE OF BIRTH ———————————————— BIRTHPLACE

DIED ———————————————— WHERE

SPOUSE

DATE OF BIRTH ———————————————— BIRTHPLACE

DIED ———————————————— WHERE

Children & Grandchildren

NAME	SPOUSE

CHILD'S NAME	CHILD'S NAME
CHILD'S NAME	CHILD'S NAME
CHILD'S NAME	CHILD'S NAME

NAME	SPOUSE

CHILD'S NAME	CHILD'S NAME
CHILD'S NAME	CHILD'S NAME
CHILD'S NAME	CHILD'S NAME

NAME	SPOUSE

CHILD'S NAME	CHILD'S NAME
CHILD'S NAME	CHILD'S NAME
CHILD'S NAME	CHILD'S NAME

Children & Grandchildren

NAME	SPOUSE

CHILD'S NAME	CHILD'S NAME
CHILD'S NAME	CHILD'S NAME
CHILD'S NAME	CHILD'S NAME

NAME	SPOUSE

CHILD'S NAME	CHILD'S NAME
CHILD'S NAME	CHILD'S NAME
CHILD'S NAME	CHILD'S NAME

NAME	SPOUSE

CHILD'S NAME	CHILD'S NAME
CHILD'S NAME	CHILD'S NAME
CHILD'S NAME	CHILD'S NAME

Reflections On Our Family Life

You are invited here to record your thoughts about your family life in general. The happiness that arose within the family should not be forgotten, for it points to a reality greater than any individual could experience in solitude. These are the times from which we want others to learn. These are the times we so greatly appreciate…

_____

_____

_____

_____

_____

_____

_____

_____

_____

Part Two:

A Time To Mourn

"Let tears flow of their own accord:
their flowing is not inconsistent with inward peace and harmony."
—Seneca

Healing the Heart

"The heart has its reasons which reason does not know."
Blaise Pascal

It has been said that time is the greatest physician. Though an ancient truism, the statement means little when we are faced with the immediacy of our own great sorrow over the loss of one dear to us. For the bereaved, the time is now and the pain is palpable. One is not able to mend a broken heart as a farmer mends a fence, that is, with a precise and long ago learned know-how that ensures a sturdier boundary line, a better fence, all within a given period of time. No, grief is not a project, but a process. The French philosopher Gabriel Marcel once said, "Life is not a problem to be solved but a mystery to be lived." And so it is with our grieving. We must somehow learn to live the mystery of it, for our balm is life itself. And the heart is bound to take us places we did not expect to journey and out of which we may not know how to escape. Perhaps the most we can do is learn to trust the heart's own reasons, which reason does not know. The heart, like a wounded animal, seeks sanctuary. It longs for a suitable refuge wherein it may find its own healing powers, a refuge wherein it will, in time, create new boundaries built of love, a love reconditioned to aim once again outward toward any number of fortunate recipients.

Some years ago Dr. Elisbeth Kübler Ross, through interviews with the terminally ill, found almost by accident the path the human heart seems to travel, with much individual variation of course, when confronted with great loss. Her findings are by no means the be all and the end all of research concerning matters of grief or loss for human beings. But what she found fit so well the emotional struggles of so many, that her model or "stages" of grief have since provided the bereaved a kind of regional map of the manifestations of their own sorrow. The stages do not treat grief as a "problem to be solved," but rather as a "mystery to be lived." They track the course of human grief in a way that can be of great aid and comfort as one finds oneself on that very course. For this reason we present here a brief overview of these stages in the hopes that you or your family members may better understand how very human is your state of being following great loss. It is our hope as well that, though you are changed forever by your loss, you can go on to live your life fully and with inspiration, meaning and love.

Grieving

In times gone by common sense told us many things about ourselves that modern scholarship is just now beginning to verify scientifically. Modern science tells us, for instance, that grieving over the death or illness of one close to us is a "natural" process. Psychologists tell us that one of the more important elements in healthy grieving is the presence of a belief system that gives meaning to suffering and death. We know that suffering and death not only have meaning but are at the core of our understanding and experience of life itself. Life teaches us that to endure the inevitable trials and sufferings of our existence is to somehow transcend it.

Rites of burial and funeral proceedings down through the ages have recognized the needs of the bereaved. But as cultures and societies change, so do some of our expressions of belief about death. In the fast pace of modern "mobile" society we sometimes forget how the comfort and closeness of family, of friends and of memorial observance united us in ways that made our suffering more bearable, the pain of tragedy less incisive, the pangs of loss and terrible sorrow of death less devastating.

Reliance upon our friends and family does not, however, eliminate our sorrow, our pain, our soul sickness over the loss of a loved one. Rather, their comfort and love infuse our suffering with meaning. Our natural longing to be with a loved one who has passed away, or our longing to have them return to us is a model of how we should strive for goodness and kindness in our lives. Our deceased loved ones remain in our hearts just as goodness dwells within us. We will still undergo the natural stages of grief that have been described so well in recent years. But behind each grief-stricken instinct is the knowledge that death is not in vain, but rather that our suffering, our grief, will find objective meaning in the time to come, specifically in our relationships with those around us.

The Stages of Grief

Most discussions on the stages of grief owe at least in part to the work of Dr. Elisbeth Kübler-Ross who, after working with terminally ill patients, began to record their fears and frustrations, their anger and anxiety, their dreams and their hopes and their manner of coping with the final stages of life. She found that the dying had much to teach the living.

Denial

What the terminally ill patient experienced was the grief attendant to his/her own imminent death. And we have found through observation that the same kinds of things are experienced by those grieving the loss of a loved one.

Of course, the circumstances surrounding the death of a loved one affect tremendously the way in which the family deals with their loss. The sudden and tragic death of a child elicits a different response than the expected passing of a grandparent who has led a long and productive life. But death, in and of itself, holds the power to strike at our hearts and cause us to recoil in disbelief. In fact a common immediate response to news of the death of a loved one is denial. Denial is a natural human response which helps to shield us from the emotional devastation that can come from tragic and/or sorrowful news. It would be common, for instance, to hear a grown son say, upon hearing of the death of his mother, "I know Mom has passed on, but I just can't fully believe that she is not with us; that if I went to her house right now, she wouldn't be sitting at her kitchen table reading as she so often did." Losing someone so dear is literally unbelievable. Gradually, however, the reality of death sinks in; but that reality is or can be mitigated by our commitment to pass on the positive lessons of the life that just left us.

Anger

It is also quite normal for the grieving family to feel anger over the loss of their dear one. With whom are we angry? At our loved one for leaving us? But that's not being fair to the memory of the deceased, is it? Well, maybe we are being too hard on ourselves. With whom are we usually the angriest—isn't it someone near and dear to us? Temporary anger is a natural part of the process. In this light, even anger at the deceased is understandable and completely human.

Perhaps we are angry at the prospect of death itself. Sometimes it seems so terribly unfair, so randomly destructive, so wantonly mad. How can it be that children of loving parents are suddenly orphaned because of a tragic event no one can explain? How can it be that such good people die so young, before their mark is fully made, before their love felt widely enough? How can it be that one of us must travel the rest of this sometimes bumpy road alone, without the usual aid and comfort of a life companion? Indeed there are so many questions death poses to us. And it can be an excruciating realization that to so many of these questions the simple answer is: *We just don't know.*

But we will eventually know if our anger is left unexpressed or unattended to, for it will resurface in ways that can be most unhealthy. First we must recognize the anger that tears away at us and know that it is a natural feeling that can, if channeled wisely, help us walk through the stages of grief to wholeness. Knowing and accepting our anger for what it is, a natural and temporary coping mechanism, is essential to the grief process. Denying our anger ensures its eventual return on a more destructive level; whereas, discussing our feelings with a spiritual advisor or a counselor can help us get beyond it. Perhaps we will try taking our anger to an understanding friend or professional, or even a group of others in bereavement.

We certainly need not be alone with such charged emotion, for those who have walked our path may understand us in a way few others can.

Bargaining

Terminally ill patients reach a point where they instinctively, out of the will to live, begin to bargain, usually with the God of their understanding. The plea may be "If only you would save me, . . ." The family of the dying patient wishes to make similar deals — it is a desperate (but so very human) effort to change what we cannot. This bargaining stage infiltrates the grieving process in that we may begin to make demands upon those around us because we feel we've been cheated of our loved one's presence. The cold realization that we cannot bargain our loved one back into existence, that we cannot wake from this dream wherein life has been altered so drastically for us is too much to handle. So the tendency to try to make a deal, with a deity, with Life itself, with people such as doctors, friends, etc. is a natural outgrowth of denial. The logic of the principle of cause and effect now seems completely illogical. We may think: " I have tried my best to live well, why then is my family being subjected to this emotionally devastating series of events? Why is this happening to me and to my family? I seem to be able to fix other things in my life, why can't I fix this? If I could only do these certain things or behave in this certain way, won't the pain of my loved one's death go away? Won't everything just be different when I wake up one morning?"

Sometimes we may decide to go to great lengths to force changes in our lives for which we may not be ready. We do so in an effort to alleviate the great loss we have suffered. But in the end the only bargain is living through what we are meant to live through. Then and only then will we know the natural and gradual release from the deep sorrow that has so overtaken us now.

And along the way we will usually find friends and other loved ones who really do know the depths to which our bereavement can take us. And even as we bargain, or try to make deals, love deepens and begins to see us through.

Depression

As our denial and anger subside, and as our notion of what we can change and what we cannot becomes clearer, a powerful and real sense of loss can overwhelm us. We become engulfed in memories of the life we led with our dearly departed loved one. We find it hard to muster any energy or respond with any sense of enthusiasm to the many kindnesses shown us. Our sadness becomes even heavier.

People have described depression in many ways. Some say it is *frozen anger*. The anger that has not been channeled appropriately or assimilated in a healthy way remains to wreak havoc in our hearts. Some say in depression it feels like we are just shutting down, that we are withdrawing from life itself, closing the doors to our soul that once welcomed in positive thoughts and ideas, as well as people close to us. Some say depression keeps one from focusing on any direction, like a traveler on a traffic circle who keeps turning down streets only to find dead ends. Despair lurks in the shadows and the world closes in. Depression can be frightful and crippling. And we would do well to recognize its destructive power.

Yet it is during this phase of grief, this depression, that love can enter our lives in a much deeper way, for it is during this heart-breaking time that we instinctively and most humbly cry out, and, in so doing, begin to tap into our innermost strengths. But the crying out is key. We need never resist the natural need to share ourselves with someone close, be it a friend or even a professional counselor. Depression is but a normal manifestation of deep mourning, a natural phase of the grieving process that will pass in time, in healthy interaction with our family and friends and with an intimate connection to the deepest part of ourselves wherein we find a strength we perhaps never knew existed.

Acceptance

If, with help, we experience these various phases of grief, but keep from becoming frozen in any one of them, then we naturally begin to accept the death of our dearly departed. Our acceptance is drenched in pain, for we have loved strongly; it is covered with sorrow, for we have given our heart and received the heart of another; it is riddled with remorse, for we feel the agonizing incision of loss; and yet we accept.

Somehow we have learned to keep on living. Maybe it was a trusted friend who helped see us through the toughest moments. Maybe it was a spiritual life we tapped into that gave us comfort. Perhaps our survival instincts came together to fashion a new way of living, living with loss but also with the joy and the peace that a good life offers. We must keep in mind that any stage of grief may return in a less intense form, and we must be prepared to cope, having learned much about living with loss in the last few months. But as each episode occurs, we feel a bit stronger, a bit more able to endure. And endure we do, by taking what we have learned and reaching out to another human being.

We begin to live with the hurt, to interpret our suffering in light of what we can do to ease the suffering of others. We draw nearer to those who offer their love genuinely. We reach out, we remember, we pay homage, we love, we live on.

Finding Help
Within the Family

As we pass through the natural stages of the grieving process an overwhelming sense of loneliness can and often does overtake us. The feeling of being isolated from even those we are normally close to is stark and very real. If we are to proceed through the anger, the depression or the other natural manifestations of our grief we have to, at some point, reach out to those around us who care about us. These caring people are often found within our family. Though sometimes family members can be too close to provide the right kind of comfort or consolation, quite often only a family member has an actual feeling for the depth and complexity of our emotion surrounding the death in the family. This empathy can be of great help if we can but open ourselves to it. It may take prying ourselves from self induced solitude to merely be in the presence of one with whom we have a shared history and a measure of understanding. Sometimes help comes from a distant family member or one with whom we never formed a bond for some reason. All of a sudden we hear from people with whom we had felt little in common and now we find ourselves accepting an invitation to have coffee with them. Something in each one's heart reached out and found a sympathetic confidant. In a way a new life of friendship begins to form in the very shadow of death.

So each family comes together as it can, some cohering in a fiercely close bond, some keeping an emotionally remote distance, but still attempting to communicate warm and heartfelt regards. Whatever the form of familial relationships, somewhere in the mix of family is usually some hidden help in hard times. Why not tap this loving resource for the relief and support we all seek in the midst of our distress? It could be a very good idea.

Finding Help Outside the Family

There are times, even in the closest of families, when it is more appropriate to seek guidance outside the family unit. At times the very closeness of the family can hinder an individual's passing through each of the stages of grief in a suitable manner. The phrase "you can't see the forest for the trees" fits here. If you have grown up in an especially close family you know how sometimes an outsider, even a perfect stranger, might be a better suited person in whom to confide when deep distress and sorrow have engulfed the family.

Fortunately, today, many funeral homes, as well as social and private agencies, conduct bereavement groups. Here one may share personal grief with others who are going through it, but without the added complexity of familial relationships that can sometimes render the weight even heavier. Attending a group of this sort is in no way a denial of the important and meaningful role the family plays in comforting its own, nor is it a sign of an inability to foster the inner strength to face life's difficult times. Rather, attendance in a bereavement group can actually become a way in which bereaved individuals can demonstrate their compassion for fellow sufferers, and thereby tap into their individual wells of inspiration and generosity of spirit.

Our Own Inner Resources

Whether we receive personal help from family members, friends, professionals or other caring individuals outside the family, help will come. And the help that will visit us has as its aim the uncovering of our own inner resources. There is an uninhabited internal landscape that slowly becomes visible to us as we cope with the deep wounds of loss. Gradually the rent heart mends itself. It will never be the same, nor should it be, for it is in reflecting upon its own experience that it grows ever larger, to the point where it becomes a meaningful resource for others. And slowly the inner landscape is dotted with people who have their own sorrow laden needs, people who cry out for someone who understands the pangs of loss. And we are that someone. Grief is changed by an outstretched hand. Because of those we have lost and those we comfort, we will never be the same.

All Grief is Special

Just as every life is an individual life, so is every death individual. And because every passing is acutely individual, it stands to reason that every grieving is as individual as the one who goes through it. Each bereaved person filters the experience of grief through their own personality and through their own personal experience. Each person brings their particular belief system to bear on the matters at hand. And this is as it should be. But the individual's personality, experience and beliefs are not the only variables in the grieving process. Who it was that passed away and the way they passed are also important determinates of how we experience grief.

Experiencing the sorrow that accompanies the death of a loved one is always difficult. But because each type of relationship with a loved one has its own unique characteristics, we may go through emotions associated with that relationship as we journey through our grief. The following section takes a look at the particularities of various kinds of grief dependent upon who it is that has passed away. It is not inclusive of every situation but is meant rather to empathize with you in whatever situation you find yourself, whether as a widow, a bereaved parent, a saddened grandchild or in any other relationship to the deceased.

Just as you bring your own individuality to the place of sorrow, you also bring that individuality to the "living through" process, the same individual strength that has seen you through other of life's trials. In this section it is our hope to tap into that very personal strength as we reflect on many of the very personal experiences of grief.

The Loss of a Spouse

If you have been "as one" in marriage, then, with the death of your spouse, a huge part of yourself is gone now, too. The grief is palpable and your best friend and confidant is not there. Those widowed know a loneliness others can't imagine. How is it possible to go on alone? How is it done?

The grief of the widowed is an immediate, intimate grief that cannot be explained or even described, only lived through with care and respect. Even as others attempt to help, the feelings of betrayal may come. How could a spouse leave, with so much living yet to do? How can I be left alone like this?

Just as grief is a process, so is learning to live again after the death of one's spouse. The deepest part of yourself has been violated and the result is an intensity of feeling that is overwhelming. The stages of grief are felt deeply. The depression and the anger are particularly hard for those recently widowed. Recovery becomes almost a form of art in that living through the grief is a very conscious effort. Acceptance of the death of a spouse and a subsequent new way of life, with a corresponding new identity does not just happen. It is crafted with the help of those who understand and those who love you.

Opening one's heart to help is not only essential, it is also the height of courage. Life will go on and you will find reason and purpose once more, but these adjustments take place at your own pace. Grief is, indeed, individual. You may have a need to seek out a support group. There are a growing number of bereavement and specifically widow/widower support groups that can be of great help. However you find your way, you will realize that your experience can benefit others. It may be through your witness of strength in a support group or your quiet understanding of another family member's pain. And as you reach out, a new life begins to unfold. Though the memory of your spouse is intact, somehow a spiritual commitment to keeping on also, alive and hopeful, proves that even a broken heart can grow larger.

The Loss of a Parent

Someone once said that parents are what stand between ourselves and mortality. After the death of a parent there seems to be a more realistic notion of our journeys here on earth, their brevity and their swiftness. The death of a parent may come as an overdue blessing or an unexpected trauma; therefore each death dictates to some extent the tenor of the accompanying grief. We may have lived far away, having had too little contact or we may have had to play the role of caregiver to one or both of our parents in their later years. We may regret that we have left unfinished business with our parent. We may find ourselves struggling with forgiveness. We are surprised at the long buried memories that surface, some perhaps sweet and radiant, some perhaps disturbing. We may have to attend closely to a surviving parent in such a way that we feel our grief being suppressed by the obligations of the time.

These are only some of the possibilities that we may encounter when we are facing the demise of mother or father. We carry a deep emotional connection to our parents that death does not destroy. Whatever the circumstances, this particular grief, more so than any other, must be a time of healing. The connection is not lost, it is changed and in the changing, it becomes more uniquely ours. It is this on-going bond that determines the way we memorialize our parents. A common way, if we have our own children, is to tell stories and recollect meaningful or entertaining times. In this way we help create the images of our parents our own children will carry with them throughout life. We may discover our siblings in a new light. We empathize with them in ways none other could. We may also seek the solace that friends, neighbors or others can provide. We may be surprised at the impact of this death. Again, it is a time for gentleness and healing. Grief occurs even when we may not think it is occurring. We listen to our own hearts and we forgive. We listen to our own hearts and we share what we have heard with someone, now or later, who we know is feeling the same confusion, anger, relief, or just plain sadness we have experienced. And we learn that love is always the answer.

The Loss of a Child

What loss can be greater than the loss of a child? When any child dies we certainly feel "diminished" as in no other way, for a child's life is meant to stretch out beyond the day, and continue in its natural cycle of growth and maturity. This life is supposed to go on and give us the satisfaction of watching the marvelous handiwork of humanity unfold before us in beauty and wonderment. So how can so tragic a thing as this be? Some people blame themselves, some blame God. But the efforts of finite minds cannot but fall short of understanding. So how are we to face life with a seemingly unbearable death? How can life ever again bring a sense of joy?

We trudge through this great sorrow sometimes an hour at a time and we feel as if we live in slow motion. The rituals we have enacted for other deaths in the family, such as the visit to the graveside, the keeping of a photograph album or the telling of stories about the deceased now are even more painful, but no less necessary to the grieving process. Some families have found solace in the establishment of funds or memorials that pertain to the life of young people, such as a school endeavor or a fund especially for childhood diseases. Gestures of this kind are anything but empty. They can resonate for years to come in positive ways for family members.

Love slowly embraces our torn hearts and begins the long and difficult road to acceptance. We may find ourselves avoiding children, to keep from breaking down. Our sorrow may be unimaginably intense. But we must hear with our hearts in this distressed time, for there are others who have experienced something akin to our pain and we may need to seek their presence if not their counsel. Ask your funeral director, pastor, neighbors or other family members if they know of support groups for those who have lost children. There is a growing awareness of the efficacy of such groups. In time, because a child's heart has become so deeply embodied in our own, we are able to help someone else whose sorrow and loneliness is all but overwhelming. And in that moment our little one's heart has come to life in a new and unique way!

The Loss of a Sibling

When a sibling passes away we sometimes find ourselves returning to the days of childhood, not only in memory but also, to a certain degree, in our emotional lives. We feel a sense of unfairness when a younger sibling dies and with one older we may have a sense of loss similar to the losing of a parent. Family dynamics are always in some state of flux, but this wound affects the whole system of family relationships in sometimes confusing ways. One sibling may have been the peacemaker in the family, another the main caretaker in regard to our parents. A death among siblings can shake the foundation of these established roles. Some siblings have stayed closer over the years than others and these brothers or sisters may now have to look to others for support and comfort.

Obviously, this is a time when families can demonstrate their unity or renew a unity that may once have existed. Often weakened family ties have been refashioned due to the shared, collective processing of the grief over a sibling's death. But within every family there will arise the pockets of loneliness that must be attended to. In honor of the deceased, new and helpful alliances may form that actually give strength to individual family members.

But it should not be surprising or considered in any way disloyal to feel the need for counsel from outside the family. Friends from work or the community may be better confidants than family members with whom we have had little close contact. Nor should we be surprised if "childlike" feelings re-emerge as we grieve our brother or sister's passing. Reason must recognize these feelings for what they are. The child inside of us is demanding attention. But remember, it is the adult who tends to the childlike feelings, therefore we do so with care and with a respect for what once existed in the life of our family. And in this way, we truly honor the memory of dear brother or sister who has gone on.

The Loss of a Grandparent

In coping with the death of a grandparent we are also coping with our culture's tendency to diminish the importance of life. Modern society evidences a remarkable lack of respect with regard to the dignity of older people. So as we participate in the arrangements of our grandparent's funeral we are forced to review the difficulties he or she encountered in the process of getting old in modern America.

We may encounter feelings of guilt for our own lack of participation in this unique life. Perhaps we have lived away and lost some of the emotional connection we once had. Perhaps our grandparent had moved on to a nursing home, had dealt with a series of sad declines in health or had gone down hill after the death of their own spouse. These are realities of modern life and death for the aged. We may also begin to remember our own childhood in which our grandparents may have played a role. We have most likely idealized this time and now we long for the warmth, security and simplicity of another time and place. We look at our own mortality and begin to wonder about our own "golden" years.

Even if we are relieved that our grandparent no longer suffers, still it is wise not to underestimate the impact of this death, for something of ourselves has passed, too. For this reason, this is a time of learning about grief. This may be the first time we encounter deep loss on life's terms. Grieving a grandparent can move us to a greater sensitivity to the burdens all families carry. Grief can make us more present for anyone struggling to accept the demise, even after a long and good life, of a dear loved one. We seek the solace of family, of contacts among professionals or understanding friends. We gather photographs as we gather memories, and we *memorialize* our grandparent, thereby recognizing their own special dignity, a dignity modern life may have been remiss in seeing. We come back to a kind of deep and abiding love learned generations ago in the life of our family. It is a love that will surely endure.

The Loss of a Special Relative

We have all had those relatives who have captured our hearts over the years. It might have been an uncle who had a knack for entertaining kids, an aunt whose cookies and stories we will never forget or a cousin who was more like a sibling. There was just something special about our relationship that we both knew and felt: a kindred spirit, a similar outlook, a shared way of seeing things. We enjoyed talking about the various and sundry characteristics of our respective extended families, while at the same time we cultivated traits that we each had developed outside our families. We may have shared how we each differed from our families, and in that sharing formed a bond at least as strong as familial bonds.

The void left when a special relative passes away is mightily felt and difficult to endure. Few may understand how deep the connection had been, how strong the bond. So where do we go for comfort? With whom may we now speak of this special friendship? Does anyone understand? Well, only those who also have now or had in the past the same kind of relationship with a special relative. Only they know how endearing a familial friendship can be. At some point we begin to observe closely our family members who we think may indeed have such a relationship. We naturally seek those who have been able to be very close friends with family members. Sometimes we feel these relationships are few and far between, but perhaps there are more of them out there than we may have thought at first.

We go through the grieving stages, we talk to others, we even seek similar relationships with other family members to varying degrees of success. But the bottom line is that we will always have a special place in our hearts for these special relatives, and no coping mechanism will take that away. Our special relative is and will always be, missed sorely. We live with them inside of us, their spirit helping animate us along our way, their memory forever cherished.

The Loss of a Close Friend

What is it that makes up the special quality of a close friendship? Is it a collection of shared experiences, similar ideals and values? Perhaps we first crossed paths at work or in our social or family life. A close friend seems to know us like a brother or a sister would know us. Somewhere along the line this friend was there when support or comfort or help of any kind was needed. This friend gave and kept on giving until giving just seemed the natural thing to do!

Very close friendships make for hard good-byes. We know we never matched the generosity of that special friend, though others tell us we did. We know we will miss this person in a different way than family, but in a way that stings deeply. This friend may have been a special link to pleasant memories of the past, or a refreshing surprise of our later years. The friendship may have been there for decades or have just begun its development. However it came about, it was being sustained in love, and it is that shared love that has wounded us in this person's demise.

Where do we go to find consolation? After all, it was so often this very friend who supplied that consolation! This is a time to understand the nature of friendship and reflect upon it, for it is sometimes hard to realize that others have formed bonds with friends much like the one we had formed with this dear person now gone. We may never find as good a friend, but we may express the special qualities of our friendship with others who can understand because they too have a friend like ours. Perhaps deep and abiding friendships are so natural a thing for us to seek out as human beings, more of them exist than we might think. At some point in the midst of this unique manifestation of sorrow, we must talk about the things that made the friendship what it was.

Perhaps we become a beacon for the lonely, for those who need a connection to humanity that has somehow passed them by. We know what a healthy reliance upon a friend can be. Maybe there is a child who is always left out of games or a shy person who was never able to socialize easily. Our experience may just touch one like this in a special way, for surely our friendship touched us in ways we will remember fondly for some time to come.

Who is Gone?

Who is it now that will never be again?
Is it a brother or sister, parent or friend?
Is it a child ripped from loving arms,
or an old one whose kindly charms
will sprout in memory's many meadows?
Brothers and sisters are our shadows
reaching side to side on life's cobbled way;
not -so- hidden stowaways
crouched in the saddened heart and limbs
of those who remain, whose sorrow swims
the tide of grief the long hours of the day.
Or is it mother or father whose body we lay
in earth to rest in much deserved calm?
They held us new and were our daily balm,
who we know now gave their lives for us,
who measured keenly, diligence and trust.
Or has a baby child now slipped from me,
from all my desperate hope to some eternity,
from my gathered, projected love,
to holy ground or star above?
Oh, our weakened beings cry aloud
to a captured heart, a funeral shroud!
For whom the creature was that is no more
is again in each our mindful, sore
imaginings and does surely now reside,
ever close in spirit, ever by our side.
                              —*John Sidney Tighe*

How We Lost Them

The manner in which a loved one has passed away has everything to do with the kind of grief we subsequently experience. The various stages of grief represent commonly shared ways of coping with great loss, but the particular context of that loss also affects us in highly individual ways. Here we briefly examine ways of coping with our loss depending upon the circumstances of the demise of our loved one. Of course there is something uniquely personal in all experiences of grief in that no individual response is an exact replica of any other therefore no two individuals react identically to loss. But however the death has occurred, there are threads of empathy to be discovered by opening our hearts to others who have been wounded by the loss of one dear to them.

A Vigil Kept

When a protracted illness envelops the life of a family and their friends, the wear on each human spirit can sometimes be devastating. Forbearance is a virtue that certainly comes into play and is the challenge of each individual who becomes a caregiver in such a situation. To witness death in slow motion can be practically unbearable. But somehow, we do it anyway; we stay the course and give what aid we can, learning the hard way that death can be the height of mercy and peace.

Sometimes long illnesses can be financially overwhelming for a family. These wounds can bring out the worst in us if we do not proceed cautiously. Many times a financial advisor can be of help when the medical or nursing care bills are growing. There are an increasing number of professionals specializing in these areas today. This may well be a time to look at possible financial options.

A long illness can also be physically and emotionally wearing upon family and friends. Having someone to talk with about what the family is going through is paramount. This may be a professional in such matters such as a psychologist or other counselor; it may be a member of the clergy trained to help with human problems that manifest their spiritual nature or it may be a caring friend in whom we have great confidence.

One thing we found in this painful process was how to recognize the special moments when our loved one either consciously or unconsciously taught us great lessons. It may have been a special gesture to a child, a small utterance of wisdom about the past life of the family, a forgiving nod or perhaps a glance that seemed to come from another world. We may or may not have had those special moments with our loved one. If we have, we cherish them; if not, we still know that our vigil kept, somehow in the big picture of things, was good and right and giving. And we learn that as difficult as suffering is, it does have meaning and will continue to be the foundation for goodness in our lives.

A Natural Course

Medical technology has not only made astounding progress in battling the effects of many once debilitating and fatal diseases, it has also extended our life spans considerably in the last fifty years. This wonderful progress, however, has created at times bewildering end-of-life issues. When once an elder may have died of what was called "natural causes" most likely in their own home, today the hospital has become the common locale of the passing of our family members and friends. Quite often last days are spent in a painless, to be sure, but drug clouded haze of medical machinery and institutional atmosphere. This all too common set of circumstances makes it all the more important to bring to one's passing a sense of human dignity, a realization that even the pain of living and of dying has redeeming qualities that live on in loved ones.

And when one we love has lived long and the natural course of events has escorted them to life's end, we must look beyond the seemingly unnatural departure modern society has created and give thanks for a long life, perhaps one that allowed for a wisdom only years can bring, perhaps for the experience of grandchildren in one's life and other joys that are possible in the golden years.

And our gratitude for the life of an elder who has passed will be noticed by others, especially the younger members of the family. To plant with them the seed that says cherish life in all its forms is an invaluable gift to enjoy, even in the midst of sorrow and grief.

A Sudden Blow

Death is rarely welcomed, but it is many times expected. It may be because of a serious illness evident in our loved one's life or the natural course of time. Families sometimes see warning signs, especially in the case of the older members. But sometimes death comes as a complete and jolting surprise. Perhaps a young person in the prime of life is suddenly struck down or a tragedy of inestimable proportion wounds a family and its friends as deeply as one may be wounded. The shock of such a death is a part of the grieving process that may not be present when a death occurs another way. The questioning of it becomes almost obsessive yet everything remains shrouded in mystery. For loved ones there is little to hold onto except each other. With sudden tragedies families must put aside differences and bond together, using each other's strength as perhaps an only defense against the pain of such profound sorrow.

But even in the absence of such care we must find a way to cope. There may have been so much left unsaid, so many hurdles left yet to the relationship with the deceased. Where do we take this residue of agony? We search our spiritual lives for the help we need and the results of that search direct us onward. We search our hearts for some manner of expressing the void left in our life. And if that search is not clouded by inordinate self-centeredness it will bear fruit in expression that might just help someone else cope with the self-same tragedy.

There is no way around feeling our heart break. But with the broken heart is a sense of what others have felt before us and what others will feel when a sudden blow strikes at a loved one. We may be their only refuge, a true refuge because we understand this special wound and we are willing to hold another's hand as they walk through it.

A Special Circumstance

There are some tragedies in life that bear with them an added hurt. Be the pain due to controversy, violence, despair or other confounding circumstances, it can be extremely intense and unsettling. Sometimes the death of a loved one carries this added weight, and so too do we carry the weight in our grief. The violence in our schoolyards, the stinging tears of heartbreak over a suicide, the devastation Nature herself sometimes unleashes, the tragedy of disease as in an AIDS related death, the pure sadness associated with a stillbirth or miscarriage — all of these special circumstances and more bring with them a burden beyond the grief itself.

As every situation is unique, so is every manifestation of sorrow and every living out of the grieving process. With any of a number of special circumstances, anger may plague the family or friends in grief. We may be angry at society for its insensitivity to the situation, at friends for not understanding, at ourselves for what we perceive we might have been able to do and even at the deceased for leaving us in such a fashion. These forms of anger are common and may perhaps play a larger role in the grieving process when special circumstances are present. Special circumstances can also bring a sense of irrational guilt. We image some solution we could have engendered but did not, when reason would tell us that basically there was nothing we could have done.

There is no "solution" to living with the grief of a death that has occurred as a result of a special circumstance. The human heart is embattled and we incur the wounds. This is a time, however, when helpful professionals may come to our aid, for the maze of sad bewilderment can lead to great depression. It is essential to cry out for help to the people we trust, and perhaps even to professionals who have dealt with these matters before. Support groups have been of great help to many in such difficult times. We know we must live this mystery, but we must also find a way to live with the future possibility of a return to peace and even the joy we deserve as a member of the human family. Be gentle with yourself; it is a time for great care.

A Distant Light

When one we care about is at death's door, we instinctively go to them. We offer at the very least our presence for them and for the rest of the family and friends. And yet, there are times when situations prevent our being there. Perhaps we live across the country and cannot get to the bedside in time; perhaps the death is as a result of a sudden tragedy and we are unable to be with family and friends for the funeral; perhaps special circumstances call for the need to refrain from being there. The distance, for any reason, seems unbearable. There is an inability to make the sorrowful situation real. One feels disembodied, separated from that which is essential. Indeed, not being present goes against our instincts and wreaks havoc with us emotionally.

Where do we turn? How do we cope with the void? What do we do? We turn to friends or counselors or clergy or some other understanding persons who can empathize with us. This need not be kept inside, for we feel isolated enough as it is. We cope by memorializing this loved one we could not be with. We do this by remembering, perhaps in journal form, our connection. We might also talk to those who were present and share with them the same kinds of things we would share if we had been able to attend. We try to break the distance down, even a little, through communication and long distance care. What do we do? We cherish the memory of our loved one. Love and memory have no physical bounds; they travel the world and touch far away hearts. Even though a distance has made the mournful time even more so, still love shared is a distant light that may help someone lost find their way.

Part Three:

Seasons of Feeling

"Life is not a problem to be solved,
but a mystery to be lived."
—Gabriel Marcel

Monthly Meditations

Each and every month something comes up to remind us of our deceased loved ones. It could be the radical individuality of the first snowflakes of December or the early spring brightness of daffodils in April. Mother Nature brings to mind the love we have shared and the people we have shared it with. In this section we want each month's reminders to be channeled into loving, caring action. We want to use the healthy forces of nature to help us be truly present to those around us. Grief has the tendency to become trapped inside our psyches, when the same potentially destructive power can be moved to project outward, moved to goodness, moved to the aid of another who may need our experience, our strength and, most of all, our hope.

This is not to say that sometimes solitude, properly experienced, is not a natural and healing part of the grieving process, for it certainly can be. It is to say, however, that the deepest part of our selves encountered in solitude or in pain, can surface to be of good, and that even loneliness, paradoxically, can be shared. And as it is shared, it begins to wane, and as it wanes we begin to see more clearly, weary as we are, the hope that does truly exist. We find that the way we came to this place of hope was through stretching a hand outward to our fellow human beings who have been or who are presently experiencing the great trial and piercing sorrow that is bereavement.

And with each month, each marked passage of time, we find it necessary to tell ourselves what we will do positively in that period to climb from the abyss of our sorrow and be of benefit to those with whom we come into contact. We affirm who we are and who we want to become as we grow through our grief.

So for each month you will find presented in this section a meditation as well as an affirmation. And with each month a beautiful illustration is offered to bring a sense of reflection and serenity to the text. Nature intended the passage of time to heal. As it heals we learn more and more that love is not bound by time. And as we heal, we defy the calendar; we go beyond this day, this week, this month.

Suggestions on Meditation

Someone once defined meditation as "doing one thing at a time". This is an easy definition to relate to in our modern world where, it seems, everyone is always doing ten different things at once. Doing "one thing" requires a slowing down, a concentrated, but relaxed focus on what lay before you. To meditate does not necessarily mean assuming a certain posture and chanting some kind of mantra for long periods of time. It does presuppose, however, that you are willing to take the time to slow down, take a few deep breaths and begin to let your thoughts venture in a certain direction, without succumbing to fretting over the hundred and one items on your daily "to do" list. To be willing to experience the healing powers of meditation is to allow a few soothing words or images to help you focus, to help you "do" one thing. That one thing may be reading or listening to music or just sitting quietly in your favorite chair, letting your thoughts tumble along like windblown leaves. Your "one thing" may even be working on a project with someone who needs your help or taking a walk in the sunshine or putting together a scrapbook of revered old photos. Meditation need not be a "sitting still" activity. But it does need to be a giving over of your worried, hurting self to the healing power residing in your own heart and mind. If you can't find the time, remember, Time exists outside of us. We humans only invented the measurement of time, not Time itself! So try taking a few minutes on a regular basis to relax and focus. Our monthly meditations may help you begin a routine of meditation. If you take the time for meditation, you will find you will end up having more time, not less at the end of your day. Try it for its healing power. Try it for yourself, you deserve it!

January

While many are making resolutions, I have learned to keep the promises at bay. Oh, I make my plans with the best of them but I no longer plan the outcomes. I try to keep myself healthy in the present; the future will take care of itself. I try to take each day as it comes. I resolve only to listen more carefully to my heart as it is renewed with the new year and as I know it will be constantly renewed all year. Who are the people who will hear the tidings of compassion that will emanate from me in this coming calendar year? Some will be family, some old friends and, of course, some complete strangers. The beginning of a new year does not automatically call for a review of days gone by or a giant to-do list for the next year. It is merely a time to take a look at the stream of my life and renew and refresh a simple, healthy sense of direction. Like the kids say, "Ready or not, here I come!"

Affirmation:

This month I won't get caught up in elaborate plans or promises. I will live in each day and take the best of each day. I will appreciate the challenge of each day by giving the challenge my heart and my will. This month I will offer a bit of myself to another. And when I am rewarded tenfold, I will not hide from the happiness!

February

I guess the world will have to be my valentine this year.
But it is a world rich with people who need friendship and
care. I have found that I am good at doing certain things
that help others. So this month is a call to think about what
I can do to make just a little bit of a difference in the life of
a family member or a friend or even an underprivileged
person in the community. Part of me has always reached
out and given something to other people. Now is no
different, though I sing with a wounded heart, there is still
a song to be sung. Who knows, even a wounded, tearful
song may be of help to someone. Love is powerful!

Affirmation:

This month I will make sure there is an outlet for my love
and compassion. Even the trials of my life can be of help,
so I will enlist them to the aid of others in need. It is in the
giving that my own pain is mitigated and put to good use.
This month I will give to others more consciously and put
my trust in my own capacity for love.

March

As winter winds itself down I look to the coming season of new growth. I am a bit frightened by the unknown, but new blossoms, colorful and fresh, dot the landscape. So many have helped me get this far, I'll just have to continue to see the beauty that surrounds me and rely on the goodness of people close to me. It is no weakness to call out for help; indeed sometimes it is a sign of strength and maturity. So as I go about my new life I make sure there is room for those who continue to be by my side, for there will be times they will need me too. And I hope to be able to be present for them as they have been for me.

Affirmation:

This month I am going to find a way to show my gratitude to those who have stayed close to me in pretty rough waters. It's usually the little things that are so meaningful, and there are a lot of little things I can do to quietly show my sincere gratitude to the good people around me.

April

With spring comes promise. The buds on the trees, the flowers in early bloom, the nearness of creation, all are inspiring. Our inner beings long for a personal springtime to mimic the earth's new vitality. We learn from Creation that new life is ever springing forth and is a mainstay of Nature herself. So it is that we are inspired to psychologically renew ourselves in the spirit of hope, to once again look with fresh eyes at the world around us and see again the beauty. Much was sacrificed so that new blossoms could flourish in the rich ground of springtime. Our suffering is not disconnected to the beauty of new growth, but rather an indelible mark upon it, ever reminding us of the great contributions of others to our well-being.

Affirmation:

This month as I appreciate the beauty of new growth around me, I will appreciate too the lives of all those who have contributed to my being able to see beauty in the world and in myself. I will speak of this appreciation to those close to me, for the contributions of those who have passed away are too important not to be shared.

May

Between the cold of winter and the heat of summer is a time of reflection, a time to peer inside ourselves, to see how we have wrestled with our pain, to see how we have positioned ourselves for the inevitable changes life brings our way. There is much to see when we have been wounded by loss. But in reflection we look out upon a meadow. We see a bigger picture; our wounds as well as the new greenness that has begun to fill out the field below us are seen in new perspective. Though each life is full of mystery, we can peer upon the known goodness a life has generated. And once we have done this, our own reflection abides in that goodness.

Affirmation:

This month I will reflect upon the goodness of my loved one who has passed away. I will not only cherish the memory of that goodness; I will try to incorporate it into my own daily living. Though I falter and succumb to my fear and my loneliness, I keep on going because the goodness brings me back to a place of hope and enlivens me over and over again. This month I will give in to the goodness that I find upon reflection.

June

There is an excitement about this month that perhaps harkens back to childhood days when school let out and shoes came off and kids went exploring in the pleasant idleness youth affords. Of course we cannot recapture those days and that time, but we can appreciate the time of year with a more childlike acceptance of the losses we have endured and the triumphs we have enjoyed. When we reflect upon childhood we sense the great trust in life and the future childhood so often holds. Sometimes, the vision of a child is like a well marked grassy lane between rows of trees, looking with hope towards a providential future.

Affirmation:

This month I will meditate on the gifts of childhood. I will attempt to see certain things with childlike eyes and thereby experience the joy and acceptance, as well as the resiliency that a child experiences. There is an essential innocence in me that only needs tapping in order for me to become a more complete person with strength for my difficulties and direction for my joys.

July

What we really celebrate when we celebrate our independence as a country is our interdependence on each other as citizens. True independence is a by-product of appropriate interdependencies among people who care about each other. Groups of people defined by what they love and hold in common are called communities. It is within these communities that we find our support in times of grief and sorrow. We are grateful to the American community for our freedom, as we are grateful to the various communities of citizens with whom we share our lives.

Affirmation:

This month I will take time to reflect upon the treasure that is my country. I will also demonstrate to the people I call neighbors, that is, my community, my gratitude for their on going support. This month I will attempt to further cultivate a "community spirit".

August

The emotional hardship that grief presents to us is as draining as the lingering heat of the summer. It sometimes seems that all the energy we have has been expelled just to keep going. A cool breeze, a slice of shade or even a bit of recreation would be just the thing to provide a little relief and regeneration. Psychologically it is incumbent upon us as we travel through our grief, to find the respite that comes from a little shade, a cool breeze or a touch of child-like activity. The breeze may be a person whom we know to be a "breath of fresh air"; the shade may be an activity like a church or social club or other group of people with whom we look forward to meeting. And the recreation may simply be a carefree dream of long ago. All of us, bereaved or not, need regular stress reducing, spiritually affirming experiences with people with whom we feel comfortable.

Affirmation:

This month I will consciously look for ways to find fellowship with people. I will look for the cool breeze and the carpet of shade that give relief from the long days of summer as well as the stress-reducing activities that help to counteract the weariness of sorrow. I will find a way to relax a little and find time for my own leisure and good health.

September

September brings the very particular sensations of Fall. The clean, crisp air begins to fill us up with welcome relief from the summer's heat and thoughts that naturally seem to journey back to days gone by. In Fall's beginning we reflect upon the past. Sometimes a melancholy comes over us, a longing for the people and situations that used to give us such joy. There is nothing unnatural about these thoughts. We let them come and we let them go. Our thoughts flow as cascades, turn as leaves. We let nature affect us without succumbing to overriding sadness or depression. We allow nature to run her course through us in peace and understanding.

Affirmation:

This month I will observe the constancy and beauty of nature as I appreciate the joys of yesterday and the hope for tomorrow. I will let Mother Nature speak to me gently and with her abounding wisdom. I will not close myself up but rather venture out into the freshness of the beginning of a new season. I will admit and accept my sorrow as I cultivate hope and the promise of new and better days ahead.

October

With the changing of the leaves we tend to reflect upon the changes we have undergone and are still experiencing. It is appropriate in the Fall to meditate on the beauty nature presents to us. Even in the midst of so many changes, nature flaunts her radiance. And so have our loved ones shone in our lives. We recall the triumphs of the human spirit we witnessed in our loved one who has passed away. And we appreciate the shining, colorful moments that enriched our lives.

Affirmation:

This month I will purposefully call to mind the victories life has allowed me and all my loved ones. There have been some very good times, usually in connection with the overcoming of obstacles life put in our path. And there are victories yet left to experience. I will keep my eyes open to be of witness to the power of the human spirit.

November

We take time this month in the form of a national holiday to give thanks for the opportunities we have had and for the people who have been a part of our lives. It is certainly appropriate to step back and look at our blessings. Our country has long been a refuge for those seeking freedom, fellowship, opportunity and the peace that any measure of prosperity can bring if nurtured rightly. This is also a good time to count our personal blessings, even as we struggle with the pain of loss. For even in the losing of a loved one we can see the blessing of having been able to be a part of their life in some form or fashion.

Affirmation:

This month I will be especially cognizant of the blessings in my life. I will attempt to show my gratitude for our nation and for the special people who have been a part of my life.

December

In the frenetic madness of materialism that has come to represent the holiday season, we must find a way to recall and revive genuine friendship and generosity. We have suffered greatly this year and no presents will serve as a solution to our sorrow. It truly is better to give than to receive in that in the giving we find some good part of ourselves eager for expression. This holiday season especially should be a time to retreat from the madness and give of our very selves to those we love and to those less fortunate than we. Yes, holidays are tough on one who is grieving; there is just no way around it. But perhaps this is just the time to slow the pace for one's own good and for the ultimate good of those we know and love.

Affirmation:

This month, perhaps even as a gift to my loved ones, those here with me and those deceased, I will create for myself a saner holiday, concentrated on people I care about and not on "things". My main gift to those around me will be my presence instead of my presents!

Seasons of Feeling

Each season brings with it emotions that touch us in special ways when we are enduring great grief. It is incumbent upon us to glean from each season the best it has to offer in the way of positive, life affirming characteristics.

Winter, with its frigid face, may sometimes reflect the cold, inner numbness a death in the family has brought upon us. But winter holds also in its sway the power to blanket us with fresh pure snow, covering all the afflicted earth with brightness and hope. It has the power to regenerate lost potential, to bring a new perspective to fear and sorrow. And in the winter we participate in the holiday season. Holidays are usually hard times for the bereaved. But even in the midst of our deep heartache, the season can be experienced in a meaningful way if we allow those who love us to love us more and if we keep in our hearts the trust that a healing is taking place, slowly to be sure, but as certain as the short days of winter.

The spring literally bursts upon us with new life in the budding of flowers and the return of blue skies. This can be a hard season in which to grieve with such wonders of nature blossoming around us. Grief lay before us, heavy and dark. We take what we can from the surrounding beauty and use it to the best of our abilities, but we have no need to fabricate a joy that just does not exist in the present. Still feeling the profound tug of sorrow does not preclude taking in the rich and vibrant symbolism of the season however. As we meditate upon spring, we have a sense that this beauty will come back to mind in a fruitful way.

Summer will carry us along with it. People we know will be taking their vacations, schoolchildren will be out for the season, and thus more visible in the community. If possible it is a time to slow the pace and encounter some healthy leisure activities for the sake of body and mind. Leisure and proper rest help to heal our emotions. Perhaps even a visit to a friend out of town or a family member who lives away could be arranged. We all need to rest from the routine activities of our daily lives, even if that daily life carries with it the lingering pang of sorrow. No, we cannot make the pain go away, but we can try our best to enter back into the natural stream of life with the help of family, friends and perhaps even the summer itself.

With Fall we naturally reflect upon the winding down of life. It is as natural as the change of leaves. This incomparable beauty of nature was meant to be appreciated and this time of year is radiant. It beckons us to open our hearts to the wonders of creation and give thanks for our place in the scheme of things. If we can only bind our feelings to this surrounding beauty, the suffering we have endured and are enduring may at least be lessened enough to recognize the hope that reaches out beyond this day.

Part Four:

The Way of Hope

*"Hope is the thing with feathers
that perches in your soul."*
—Emily Dickinson

The Way of Hope

There is a heartache so deep and wide
when one we love has passed away;
a rend complete and scar so hard to hide,
a lonesome path, cloud of darkest gray.

But there is a place in our suffering and woe
in stinging wound of breadth and scope,
a speck on our hearts where love can go,
a widening road we call... the way of hope.

For inside our agony is a virtue higher
so high it flies with airy wings above
the tearful, lonely and somber hour;
higher than solemn grief is selfless love.

We love the memories, this hour to keep.
Records and keepsakes their sense evoke.
Farewell dear loved one in life's great leap
upon the widening road...the way of hope.

Even when cherished memories fade
love keeps alive the ties that bind,
exposes death's dark masquerade,
for love lives on in a longing mind.

Love lives on in story and song,
in youth who toward life's fullness grope.
Loved ones live on, be life short or long,
in the inheritance of love... the way of hope.

—F. G. Beal

I walked a mile with Pleasure;

She chattered all the way.

But left me none the wiser

For all she had to say.

I walked a mile with Sorrow

And ne'er a word said she;

But oh, the things I learned from her

When Sorrow walked with me!

—Robert Browning

Journal of Hope

In this section we invite you to gather some of your thoughts in the written word, for in writing many times our thoughts become more clear, more pointed toward the good, more infused with hope.

You may want to write to yourself in an inner monologue, a good conversation with yourself about all you have been through and about the unknown possibilities that lie ahead. Or you may imagine an audience, perhaps an audience of family, years down the line reading to get a sense of who their storied ancestors were. For them you give a legacy of love and a brief but meaningful memoir of hope. Some have found great solace in actually writing to their deceased loved one, for they found a way to say what was not said before, or a way to say it more reflectively. You might even write a few pages of thanks to those who are even now standing by you.

Whatever you decide to write, however you decide to write it and, of course, in whatever time frame you choose, we are happy to provide you with a place for the inner workings of your heart to reside, a place on the page for your outstretched hand to the world.

_____

_____

_____

_____

_____

_____

_____

_____

_____

_____

_____

_____

_____

_____

_____

_____

_____

_____

_____

_____

_____

_____

_____

_____

_____

_____

_____

_____

_____

_____

_____

_____

_____

_____

Help In Bereavement

Fortunately today there is much help for those experiencing grief. Many times local funeral homes, mental health agencies, family physicians, psychologists, and church or even civic organizations have some sort of grief counseling available, either one to one or in small support groups. These people and organizations have helped thousands live with their sorrow and loss in ways that are comforting and life affirming. By drawing on the experience and empathy of others we learn to cope with loss more practically. We also learn the essential place reaching out to others in pain has in our own lives. As we join our suffering to that of others we begin to assimilate certain basic spiritual principles that have guided humankind for centuries. We begin to understand that our pain need not be in vain, that everything that happens is not necessarily random but perhaps a part of some swirling, mysterious, tragic, joyful, bewildering design that, in the end, will result in a sense of meaning, purpose and hope.

List of Helpful Organizations

The Grief Recovery Institute
An internationally recognized authority on grief recovery, with training programs, a Grief Recovery Handbook, as well as outreach, certification and community education programs.
Tel. (323) 650-1234.

GriefNet
Griefnet is an Internet community of persons dealing with grief, death and major loss. Griefnet also operates a companion site, KIDSAID. KIDSAID provides a safe, on line place for kids and their parents to find information and ask questions concerning loss and grief.
www.GriefNet.org

The American Hospice Foundation
The American Hospice Foundation aids programs that serve the needs of the terminally ill and grieving individuals of all ages. Initiatives include: guidance for caregivers of the terminally ill, educational campaigns to aid bereaved employees and co-workers, training and materials on grieving for teachers and school counselors, educational programs for clergy and workshops for hospice staff and others serving grieving families.
Tel. (202) 223-0204.

The Funeral Service Education Foundation
This division of the National Funeral Directors Association has information and resources on bereavement issues as well as other grief related materials. Tel. (877) 402-5900.

GROWW
Grief Recovery On-Line (GROWW) is dedicated to providing support and assistance to people who have lost a loved one to death. The workplace of GROWW is the Internet. www.GROWW.com

Renew: Center for Personal Recovery
Specialists in crisis management for schools and other organizations. Renew offers services for individuals, families and organizations experiencing any kind of trauma or loss. Educational resources and workshops available.
Tel. (859) 986-7878.

WidowNet
An Internet information and self-help resource for, and by, widows and widowers. Topics covered include grief, bereavement, recovery and other information helpful to widows and widowers.
www.fortnet.org/WidowNet

The Compassionate Friends
A self help support organization designed to assist families in the positive resolution of grief following the death of a child and to provide information to help others be supportive.
Tel. (630) 990-0010.

SHARE
SHARE's mission is to serve those who are touched by the tragic death of a baby through miscarriage, stillbirth or newborn death. Web site offers packet of grief literature, information on local chapters, bimonthly newsletter, resources.
Tel. (800) 821-6879 or (636) 947-6164.

National Sudden Infant Death Syndrome Resource Center
NSRC provides information services and technical assistance on sudden infant death syndrome (SIDS) and related topics. The mission is to promote understanding of SIDS and provide comfort to those affected by SIDS through information sharing. Tel. (703) 821-8955.

Survivors of Suicide
SOS is a bereavement support and information division of the American Association of Suicidology, an organization that is dedicated to the understanding and prevention of suicide. Tel. (202) 237-2280.

The National Organization of Parents of Murdered Children
POMC is the only national helping organization which is specifically for the survivors of homicide victims and which follows up with supportive family services after the murder of a family member or friend. Tel. (888) 818-POMC.

No Greater Love
A humanitarian organization dedicated to providing annual programs of remembrance, friendship and care for families who lost a loved one in the service of our country or by an act of terrorism.
Tel. (202) 783-4665.

The Healing Word

As human beings, language is our primary means of communication. When we experience elation or fear or sadness or sympathy, we communicate these emotions through language, often the spoken word we use in much of our daily life. But we also encounter the utility and purposefulness of language in the written word. For some their bible is the truest comfort of life. For some the stories of great authors fill a void that gives meaning to life. And for some casual reading helps them escape the daily tensions and the ups and downs of modern living. We read because we are communicating animals and our souls need the mental and spiritual nourishment that inspiring and insightful words can provide. When we read we are actively searching our imaginations to reach the author on some common ground of understanding and empathy. It is as if our very beings call us to this activity.

In our grieving too, the act of reading can play an important role. We read what others have experienced. We read of hope and the resiliency of the human spirit. We read about practical ways to cope with what has happened in our lives. And we read of a better time coming for us; we are able to see that time because someone good with the written word has agreed to help by creating a picture of a brighter tomorrow, somewhere beyond this day.